The Testers Book (Revised Edition)

An Unconventional Way to Software Testing

"The principal objective of software testing is to give confidence in the software." – Anonymous

The Testers Book
An Unconventional Way to Software Testing

A breakthrough overview of Software Testing, master the basics so you can learn it all...

Rogerio da Silva

It is published in Amazon Kindle store as eBook format, in Amazon KDP printing format, in iTunes in eBook format and Google Play.

Cover Design: Rogerio da Silva
Illustrations by: Rogerio da Silva

Dedication

Firstly, to my wife, who is and has always supported me on my craziest adventures, whom I trust to go to the end of the world, who critiques my work and helps me stay put in my goals as I'm a dream-and-ideas machine.

To my two little girls, who inspire me to keep on going, so I can build something that I know can support the family and free up time to spend with them; so I'm able to see them both growing up. I call them little scientists and little explorers as they come up with the wildest adventures, proportionally to their age (2 ½--year toddler and three-month-old baby), of course.

To my mum and dad, brother and sister, living far away (about 5k miles away), I say thank you. Even with that much distance we're still bonded, and they all support me in my pursuit to be successful. I owe a lot to them for a considerable portion of me today comes from them: respect, honesty, integrity, obeying the laws of the universe, loving nature, and being happy no matter the circumstances.

To my friends from the past and present, I got a bit from each one of them that served me in my pursuit today.

To all the difficult and challenging people, I have encountered in my work experience, without them I would not have forced myself to do my best and to get through difficult times.

To all the failures I have had in the past that have helped me build up my strength and filter out all the bad stuff and focus on the right and proper thing. To failure until you make it!

Table of Contents

Introduction

In 2009, I lost my job as a telecom engineer. I had invested time, effort and training; in my mind, I had to get courses and train to get a promotion, to ultimately, earn more money. It wasn't what I wanted in life; I've only realised that later in life.

I'm a Brazilian, expat in the UK since 2001. Within a few months, I met Daniela (half Brazilian and half Italian), who's now my wife. Since then we've lived in between Brazil, then Leeds in the UK, and briefly in Italy.

When this episode happened in 2009, maybe due to the 2008 economy house crisis; back then, unfortunately, I watched more TV and news and inadvertently I allowed all that information get into my mind, and maybe due to the missing family factor I was also reading and watching more news about Brazil. I trusted that the country was in a better position, opportunity-wise, so I could get a job there instead.

In the meantime, a friend, who lived in the UK and gone back to live in Brazil, said to me, "Rogerio, there's a computer shop, also a wholesale of parts for repairs, available for sale by an old friend of mine, and I thought of you. How about becoming partners?"

The thought of having my own business had always crossed my mind, and I thought this could be an opportunity.

Short story is, I convinced my wife that it was time to move on. She did not like the idea but supported me. We sold everything in one month and moved to Brazil, with limited savings money—the savings for a mortgage—and with the promise that it was a good business and the prospects coupled with what the news was giving about Brazil, I accepted the proposition without thinking it through.

During the 2 ½ years that I was with the business, I made wrong decisions, trusted wrong people, got into debt, and eventually we became bankrupt.

I was devastated. My wife went to a very dark place; but we stayed together all the way.

Late 2012, I did end up getting an opportunity with a local software house, wanting to expand their business as in a franchise format, providing ERP system on a SaaS basis. This was around the region we were living in: the Sao Paulo countryside. The owner trusted that I could help them in stabilizing new units throughout the small towns. That started to have a shift effect in me.

I got inspired by the opportunity and by the support I was getting, and I remember thinking, this could be my opportunity to shift things around.

I've started to learn how a real entrepreneur mindset works; understanding how the vision of the CEO, Marcelo Guimaraes, and his positive influence has impacted and added to decisions in my professional life.

He has helped me as much as he could; today his software house Gigatron Franchising is a successful brand not only in Sao Paulo state but across 17 counties. Unfortunately, I was in so much debt that I could not have done my part correctly and grow together with the company.

In the meantime, I kept in touch with friends in the UK, and up until then, Daniela and I had not admitted that we wanted to go back to live in the UK. We knew that we would have so much more opportunities and despite the economic downturn, it will still be a better place to be at that moment in time, due to the physiological factors or due to the economic factors or due to the shame from family and friends and the guilty of failing. I don't know, but I understand that it was the best decision we would have made back then.

The venture with the franchising did not last more than six months, but it did give me the foundations of being mentored by a truly successful entrepreneur, and the opportunity to learn the model itself.

When we returned to the UK in 2013, with just our briefcases packed with hope, having the opportunity of a fresh start, with the help of our friends who had to give us shelter, we were set to start over again. No matter the job I was going to get, I just wanted to work and do the best I could do.

That was when things in my way of thinking started to shift, and that's when I had begun to realize **what** I was doing, the reasons **why**, and **where** I wanted to be.

In the very next day of our arrival, I printed out some CV's and then I went to the city centre of Leeds in Yorkshire. In the very first recruitment agency I walked into, I shook hands with a recruiter who straight away, in a 5-minute conversation, offered me a job in the same area of my friend's house where we were temporally staying until we got a job and rented a flat or something like that.

It was shocking to me. I was surprised and did not overthink about what it was or meant; I just went with the flow. It was a job in customer services, in the phones and emails, for a known logistic/delivery company in the UK and Europe.

I got the job; however I was a bit nervous about the training. Primarily due to English not being my first language, even though I can speak English fluently, with a strong Brazilian/Yorkshire accent. ☺

However, like I did mention, I set my mind to do whatever I was tasked to do. By then I already started to trust the universal laws and accepted all the responsibility in the things that had happened in my life.

The journey from my friend's house to the job, even though it was in the same housing state, was a 50 minutes' walk. I could have taken a bus, but I wanted to save money so we could move to our flat.

I'm telling this story because it is relative to who I am today, hang on with me as the story gets even more enjoyable.

Around that time, I bought a new phone with Internet access and started to download and stream audios related to answering phone calls, ended up listening to sales techniques; then motivational audios; then inspirational audios; then the laws of the universe and how it works; the reasons behind the way we think; the way we do things; how much emotion affect our lives, positively and negatively depending where you are focusing on. Boom!

That was it! Every day, 50 minutes' walk. Each journey, I've listed to hundreds of audiobooks, listened to speakers in the subject, from motivational to inspirational to entrepreneurship. These made so much impact in my life and started to have a positive effect in me, with my life; letting go of the past, especially the painful ones, and having a better relationship with my wife, family and friends.

Even more so in my work, within months, I was training people, in customer services (did I mention that English is not my first language?) That was a big deal from me. Once I had gone over my blockade, this was no longer the case. I still have the strong Brazilian/Yorkshire accent, but that is not a blockade.

In a year's time, if you ask me if I was going to do that, I would say: No way!

Then I was interacting with everyone in my section, maybe because I wanted to learn. I was curious about what the business process was, how I was able to help customers and help other working colleagues, but in the same proportion, pass on the knowledge. I wanted to tell people that if you wish, you can do it—just like I am doing now. I used to say that back then, and I still say that now.

The company and the customer services' department were going through a transformation, and part of that was the introduction of a CRM system, and I was asked to participate in the UAT (User Acceptance Testing), until then I had never heard anything about the software development life cycle, even when I was working with my friends in Gigatron Franchising, perhaps because my focus was more in sales.

I of course said yes, and due to the weeks of preparation for the implementation the test manager must have seen the interest that I had, how inquisitive I was, how I was asking the questions and the understanding of the business process because I was interacting with almost everyone in the department, this surely must have had an influence in his decision and I accepted.

I've started as Junior, learning the basics, being mentored by a Master's in Software Testing and a buddy who is enthusiastic as I am, and that's when I got into Software Testing. The previous experience in computer support, computer networks (Cisco), Telecoms and the attempt to become an entrepreneur has helped with the process.

Since then, I've studied the basics, and soon later I've realised the freelance (contractor) side of the work, and I made the impossible *possible* and within a short 2 years, typically only when you are a senior level (5 to 10 years), I then migrated into that side of the fence, and since 2015 I've had the pleasure to work with different clients, in different backgrounds, with different challenges.

I've always wanted to share my experience. I have been adding information in my blog www.rogeriodasilva.com, but now I think there is time to have a step further and share in more depth, based on my past years' experience, launching my professional consulting services at a myexpert.consulting *website*.

I wanted to share not just the technical skills and qualifications, but also the soft skills and how I've overcome my fears, my limitations, my insecurities, my negative beliefs and how I became a successful tester and now earns six figures a year consulting and how you can too.

By knowing the secrets of nature's universal law and how that affects us, in whatever field you are working with, in whatever place on earth you are at right now, these fundamentals can help you succeed just like it has with millions of other people in the past.

This isn't new, and it was not invented by me. It is a historical fact. Many people have and are leveraging this knowledge right now, and I think you should too. I'm confident that it will have a profound effect in you too.

What to Expect from This Information?

Background

I have been working individually with Software Testing since 2013, but with technology (Telecoms, computer repairs, business systems such as ERP, CRM, Web Applications and more) from 2005, already having an interest before that but professionally since then.

The Objective

The aim here is to give you an overview of Software Testing, so you'll get the primary ground. If you are starting to get an interest in this field or for you who is a junior and just got into the area and want to understand a bit more of what and where to go from here.

The Technique Approach

In my experience, not just the technical skills have helped me succeed, but there are other factors, which I share embedded here throughout this book. The topics in which I give an overview that are a little bit unconventional are: 'Whom Do You Listen To?', 'Teachability Index', 'The Training Balance Scale' and 'The Four Steps to Learn a New Information'.

This type of information, I don't recall seeing in my school and college time, neither on training sessions that I've attended in the past. But stick with me, read it, and you will soon understand how much powerful this technique is and is also applicable in any other parts of your life, not just in the Software Testing career but in anything that you apply it to.

Reasons

I wanted to share because I think it is the right thing to do and because it has helped me and others that I've met within this field. By all means, this information is well applicable in everything you do in life, not just for this career.

Stick with me until the end, and you will soon realise that.

I'd Love Your Feedback

You could reach me outside this book if you wanted to know more about those topics as well, here I scratch the surface as what I intended to do here is to give you the level grounds of the potential that your journey can be.

I hope you enjoy these teachings as much as I did enjoy writing them down and shared with you.

I would like to hear your questions, thoughts and observations. Any feedbacks are more than welcome.

You can contact me directly via:

email: contact@myexpert.solutions
LinkedIn: www.linkedin.com/in/rogeriodasilvauk

Personal Blog: www.rogeriodasilva.com
Services Related Website: myexpert.solutions

There Are Two Types of Professional Testers

Before we go ahead and get deep into the contents here, I wanted to point out that there are two types of professionals, in this subject *tester*, but it is shareable with others in the same IT software development field.

Software Tester Professional #1: The Permanent Job

It is known as a long-term contract, indefinite term or fixed term contract, typically 12 months' contract with the salary based the same as a long-term contract.

The yearly salary can vary from 25K for a Junior position to a 60K for a manager or technical level (automation, performance or security tester). If you are in the United Kingdom, you can use 'The Salary Calculator' (bit.ly/2Hjltkr) website to have an idea of the take-home salary.

An individual who wants to work for a company on permanent basis, seeking job security (if you can ever call that in these days), regular pay, in most cases, monthly; with all the benefits of being a permanent member of staff—car parking, health care, dental care, training packages, cycle-to-work scheme, discounted shopping vouchers, school vouchers, holiday paid, sick day paid, and all the benefits of being under a permanent company can provide you with.

There is a career path, and you can get guidance from the senior management team and HR/Training team.

You will have appraisals, where both you and your line manager can help you set goals, objectives for the year and review them as you go along; that can help you with your job development career as well as getting the bonus if that's the case where you are.

You get to participate in important meetings and get more involved in strategic decisions.

Moreover, if this is the case and you fall into that category, by all means, keep doing that. I respect that. But if you want to be successful and excel in this field, you may consider going to the Software Tester Professional #2.

Software Tester Professional #2: The Contractor Job

It's also known as consultant or freelancer or short-term contract, varying from 3 to 6 months and rare cases 12 months' contract.

The salary is on a daily rate plus 20% VAT (for the UK, not sure about elsewhere).

It can vary from £250 to £550 plus VAT, calculating using about 220 days in a year, that includes bank holidays and a decent holiday, do the maths and you will see the differences in salary for a permanent to a contractor. If you are in the United Kingdom, you can use 'SJD Accountancy' (bit.ly/2HtxLFx) to calculate the take-home salary. (this is my accountant by the way, and if you do end up joining them, please let them know that I have referred you to them.) ☺

You would have to set up your own limited company and provide the services and invoice the company. You need to have an accountant to help with the VAT returns, accounts return, and the personal taxes, insurance number, income tax and more.

You will have to get insurance covers such as the professional indemnity insurance (PI insurance) covers against claims concerning mistakes or negligence in your work. It is also used to cover any expenses incurred in your defence. Without a doubt, a must-have. I use Hiscox UK (bit.ly/2VF2qty)

You will not get the benefits as permanent individuals do.
You will not get holidays to pay.
You will not get a sick payday.
You will not get training.
You will not get appraisals.
Also, you will not get into important company decision meetings, just in that particular project you are designated.

To become a contractor, firstly you need to be within the experience bracket, but in case you are offered from the start to be self-employed, how you choose to operate could impact your level of responsibility, the work you take on, and your take-home pay.

Your situation could fall into one of these three different routes:
#1 Limited Company
#2 Umbrella Company
#3 Sole Trader

The accountants would be able to explain in more detail as I do not qualify to expand the details on that.

The reasons why I've chosen to go self-employed:

#1 Increased take-home pay. Generally earning more than permanent work.

#2 Freedom. You have more control of when and where to work. If not happy with the project, place a 1-2 weeks' notice and the flexibility to leave without damaging your image in LinkedIn's job history and CV as is reasonable to work in short-term project contracts.

#3 Variety of work. As I have had the opportunity to be exposed to different projects, it has forced me to learn more, consequently getting more experience; therefore, becoming more marketable.

Whom Do You Listen To*?

Before we dive into the Software Testing subject, I wanted to give the fundamentals as part of the soft skills. I believe that in combining those two, technical and soft skills, you can go further.

One of the basics is that it is essential to know who you listen to.

It would be best if you focused on getting the inspirations from the person whom you would like to become in your career.

Find out the person you can learn from, how it works, how it speaks, and how it does the self-development.

I know you are probably thinking that I'm saying this, so you listen to me and follow me; but that's not the point.

The point is, successful people, do have a mentor, a coach, someone whom they can talk to and exchange and share information.

If you don't have someone in person, get a biography book. Reading is compelling, and leaders are tremendous readers.

You can get training from someone who is an expert in your field or the field that you wanted to be.

You can get to social media groups and learn from the shared information. You can hire a coach and ask the questions that you have so you can enhance your career life.

However, be very careful of whom you do listen to. It doesn't do any good if you look and copy someone who is not an expert in the field.

Is like you want to become a chef and want to make the best chocolate cake in the market, you should be learning from a master chef and not a breakfast chef who does fried eggs and microwave baked beans. You do need to get from the best.

It may cost more, more effort and more done to get that, but it does worth it as you are getting the information from the master source.

'Who Do You Listen To', the concept is not new, and is widely known from The Global Information Network, in the series 'Your Wish is Your Command', though by Kevin Trudeau a former 33 degrees member of the secret society The Brotherhood, it has been used by many people to achieve anything people wanted.

1. What is Software Testing

Software testing is an integral part of software development. It allows us to get to find about any errors, known as 'bugs' in the software so we can correct them before it released to the public. The process of software testing done by the software testers who look for all the potential defects.

Why is Software Testing Necessary?

It is necessary to verify and ensure what has been developed does what it is supposed to do. Software testing is essential to check the new functionality works as intended. A unique feature may break an existing element, by carrying out a regression test, the issue can be found before it becomes a problem and is released to the user. This is just one of the testing objectives, regardless the tests methodology applied, the aim of a software tester is to ensure what has been developed does what it was supposed to do based on business requirements.

To deliver the best application, we can. Undoubtedly, the goal is to provide an application to users so they can use the app with the best experience and quality as possible. Simple cosmetic issues such as an image or a non-well-aligned button may not be a big issue, but instances where users' privacy is compromised, or there's loss of revenue can lead to significant problems leading to loss of reputation and in extreme cases life-threatening; therefore best quality is an essential element of software testing too.

Making sure the application has the capability of having multiple users accessing the system at the same time. Something may not be prepared for significant stress or load accesses simultaneously. People can face a long loading time, unable to login, unable to book a ticket for a trip or a concert and many other similar situations. Testers can simulate this scenario, which can help identify flaws so developers can rectify it before the release.

There are hundreds of devices around the world, with different sizes, shapes, operational systems, plus there are several types of browsers—new and old, with and without proper updates—which can affect the user directly, resulting in a bad experience using the application. Therefore, software testing is necessary on cross-device and cross-browser, so developers can make adjustments to cover at least the most used devices and browsers.

Have you heard of edge case? Well, it is pretty simple. There's always someone who has the assumption that the user would never do this or that. Then, when the software is released, guess what? User does just that. Therefore, exploratory testing is as well necessary to cover and unleash just those situations when the user goes over the borders.

Software Tester

A software tester is a person who test software, web application, mobile apps and any other system used in all electronic devices for errors, defects and bugs. They also look up for different issues that can influence the execution of the program, software or an application. It would not be wrong if we say that the Software Testers are essential for the software development team. They used to perform non-functional and functional testing of different programs using automated or manual programs testing systems.

Quality Assurance

Individuals get confused about the differences of a QA (Quality Assurance) and a Software Tester. Even though they are interrelated and to some degree, they can also be considered as the same thing; yet there are few things that set them apart from each other.

Quality Assurance incorporates such techniques that guarantee the usage of processes, methodology as well as the standards to check the created program and its other expected requirements. Quality Assurance mainly focuses on procedures and strategies rather than accurate testing on the system. We can call quality assurance as for the subset of Software Test Life Cycle. Quality Assurance consists of some preventive exercises as well as the process-oriented exercises.

Software Tester applies the strategy and carries out the tests.

Manual Testing of a Software

Manual Testing is a procedure completed manually, covering what is visible on the screen, testing the functional aspect of the software to look for any defect in it. In this technique, the software tester has an essential role and checks all components of the application to guarantee that the conduct of that particular application is working as per requirements. The Manual Testing is a fundamental type of testing which finds out the bugs in the application under test.

In its preparation to test, testers must produce a test plan that leads them through a set of test cases.

For repetitive tests, it is recommended but not mandatory to apply automation tests whenever possible according with how much effort, budget, time and knowledge the software tester has. One crucial point to emphasize is the fact that applying 100% automation is not ever possible. There will always be elements that only human interaction can test, such as design, colours and functionalities that require human intervention.

A manual tester aims to position himself as a user and go through all the software usability to identify flaws in the system and in the process that can be rectified before a release.

An informal approach is to carry out exploratory tests that, in most cases, are sufficient in a development cycle. With a casual approach, testers explore intuitively and rely on its experience and expertise to gain an intuitive insight to how it feels to use the application, raising defects as it goes along to the development team to fix before its release.

Larger projects require a more rigorous methodology approach to identify and fix as much defects as possible as development goes along.

In whatever methodology applied, such as Waterfall model, Agile through Black, white or grey-box testing, the key elements recommended by ISTQB (International Software Qualifications Board) is to follow those vital elements to a successful software testing process:

Test planning and control – Planning: What, where, how, and who will test. Control: What to do when diverting from the plan. Compare and adjust the test against the project and the actual testing.

Test analysis and design – What to test or test conditions. Test cases are elements to cover the minimum level of terms as possible. That is the bridge between planning and test execution.

Test implementation and execution – Are the activities that involve running the tests. Check environment, prioritization and test cases based on analysis and design: retests and regression tests.

Evaluating exit criteria and reporting – Defined in test planning before test execution starts. Check if tests executions have met the expectations. Determines if more tests are needed. Writing test results of activities for business sponsors (PO - Product Owner and PM – Project Managers) and other stakeholders (BA – Business Analyst, TM – Test Manager, DEV - Developers).

Test closure activities – Testing has finished. Now is a wrap-up task. Reports wrote defects closed, and defects deferred to another phase logged. Close and archive test environment and write down lessons learned to improve the testing process.

Test Automation

In today's world, when everything is dashing, it is a challenge for any organization to continually keep up and enhance the quality and proficiency of the software development team. In numerous programming projects, testing ignored as a result of time or cost constraints. This results in the absence of best quality along with the client disappointment and increases on overall costs of the project.

The principle explanations behind these additional costs are usually the poor test methodology, delay in testing, consequent maintaining the test, or it may be the underestimated effort of test case generation.
Test automation can enhance the development process in many ways. For repetitive tasks and with the intention of scalability, automation is a must.

Some examples of how automation can help is when applied in regression test after debugging and fixing a bug in a software. It may uncover other parts of the software due to that fix. Also, when it comes to cross-device and cross-browser tests, it can help immensely applying the same feature in multiple places to observe the behaviour which in turns will help the team and developers make adjustments to cover as many users as possible.

Automation can be tested at:

Unit level – Unit tests are a growing trend in software development and its use of xUnit frameworks mostly used in Agile methodology, which is also known as TDD (Test-driven development). Tests are writing in units and defined before the code gets written. Trust that unit tests are better to discover errors earlier in comparison with Waterfall methodology when most of the application gets developed.

A GUI (Graphical User Interface) level – also called as record and playback which allows users to interactively records actions and reply them in a certain number of times. It can be less technical and requires less software development. It faces reliability and maintainability problems as in a minor change such as change of a text, button position or column needs it to be re-recorded and retested. For web testing, you may have heard of Selenium Web Driver which use the HTML and DOM events instead of operating system events to record and apply the test cases. Ideal for cross browsing tests. Another useful GUI automation test is the mobile testing as in this way testers can cover multiple devices inserting action in different sizes, resolutions and operating systems on smartphones.

API driven – Due to the amount of work in maintaining GUI-based automation testing, API is now widely used by software testers. As part of the integration testing, APIs can test functionality, reliability performance and security of an application. As opposed to GUI, APIs performs at the message layer level, which is considered critical when API serves as the primary interface to application logic, and GUI can be challenging to maintain short release cycles.

In summary, software testing is necessary for all development of any software. The hardest part is to find the right balance between risk, quality, budget and time.

2. Responsibilities of a Software Tester

There are various types of Software Testing individuals or Software Tester in the technology world today. There are analytical testers and technical testers. The individual chooses the route is down to the responsibilities which differ from one another in how the work is carried out. On both of the options, their duties include testing of the software and reporting any errors present in the SUT (System Under Test).

There are few different organisations which have unique arrangements of additional responsibilities given to their Software Testers. These other responsibilities assigned to them to get the best possible results regarding the software under testing.

Below are a few points of what to expect from software testers in terms of responsibilities in a typical project involved.

- Software testers should learn everything about the product under test and any other program which is related to that product.
- Software testers should completely get clarification and understand the project plan and its testing.
- Before testing, software testers should learn the product prerequisites and get clarification on all that is not clear and ambiguous requirements.
- Software testers should make their testing plan according to the requirements of the software.
- Software testers should set up the necessary testing data, application software and sufficient system to access the environment in SUT (System Under Test).
- Apply test automation whenever possible.
- Testers should register and prepare test logs.
- Report the test results to stakeholders.
- Retest all the returned bugs and close it if passed, back to the developers if persisting.
- Carry out a regression in solved bug fixes.
- Redesign test cases when finding deformities (Bugs/Issues/Defects/Undesirable behaviours) and diversions from the plan.
- Check if tests executions have met the expectations.

- Report all the progress of the work along with any issues found to the Test Lead or Project Manager as required.
- Support the group with any testing assignments.
- Stay updated on technology development as well as software testing tools.

Risks

During the process of software testing, risks are considered as an essential topic to look out for and all its obstacles to test, recreate the scenario and help team minimise or completely cease the impact before the software is released.
Risks are the likelihood of a harmful or undesirable result. It is something that has not happened yet and it might never happen. We can say that it is a potential issue.

The question: Is it more than likely to have risks in any software development? Managing risk is an essential movement in program testing, arranging and following. It incorporates the recognisable proof, investigation and treatment of dangers confronted by the business. A risk can be managed at different levels: extend level, program level, association level, industry level and even national or worldwide level.

In software testing, risks can divide into two categories.

#1. Risk about the product, including variables identifying what created.

- Defect prone software delivered
- The critical flaws in the product that could cause harm to an individual (injury or death) or company
- Poor software features
- Inconsistent software features

#2. Risk about the project which includes components identifying with the way the work is done.

- Supplier issues
- Organisational factors
- Technical issues

Analysis and Activities

During the analysis, testing team and software testers consider the prerequisites from a testing perspective to recognise the testable necessities. The QA (Quality Assurance) group may connect with different stakeholders to comprehend the requirements in detail. Needs could be either Functional as well as Non-Functional — automation attainability for the given testing product likewise done in this stage.

The activities of software testers are all those tasks which are done to test the product. These activities include:

- Finding out different kinds of tests performed.

- Gathering insights about testing requirements and core interest.
- Planning the Requirement Traceability Matrix (RTM).
- Identifying test environment objectives where testing completed.
- If required, the automation feasibility examination is also done.

In summary, testers are responsible for the quality of the end product, as well as risks that its software may perform but also is a constant help with the process improvement, providing crucial impartial evidence to stakeholders and decision-makers to achieve milestones and the conclusion of a project, then passed on to the maintenance team.

Software testing is a crucial and essential part of the development process.

3. Salary of a Software Tester

The job of a software tester is to assess the quality of software applications. They are also known as Quality Assurance. Testers are IT experts and help to validate the product in development, making sure it's practical and usable. Software testers often have a degree in computer science or IT. However, the role is open to graduates from a variety of degree disciplines. You can enter the software testing profession with an HND or foundation degree.

Companies may most highly regard a software, IT, or engineering diploma. Salary varies accordingly with experience; naturally, a junior position as tester will be equivalent to a new graduate position and increases consequently with time, certifications, and for more specifically skilled roles such as automation, security and management.

There's also the consultancy route for more senior highly skilled testers if you prefer to become self-employed with a short-term contract, instead of a fixed term or permanent settlement.

Salary Range – UK

According to a survey by ITJobsWatch.co.uk (goo.gl/KpW57u), in the year 2016, permanent software testers earned anywhere in the range of £37,000 (British Pounds) to £77,500 (British Pounds). This can vary from region to region (more important centres pay a bit more than smaller towns) and the skill set needed for a particular project. Manual testers earn a bit less than automation; the next level up would be security, engineer, then management.

In the year 2013, a junior could have started from figures around 18k to 20k, then with two years of experience or a bit less, I would say around 18 months, a tester would get to the point of about 28k to 30k a year salary. Those with two to four years of experience earned from 35K up to 40K a year.

Those having minimum five years of experience earn today no less than 40K to 45K a year, which is good and even better if in the meantime you get yourself into automation which can get you around from 45K to 60K a year, which is quite good.

Salary potential can vary from organization to organization, often is heard that game industry pays less than financial or health sectors. A web application is just as crucial to any other application, but it's classed as less critical in comparison with an ATM or life support machine. For that reason, you can add an extra 2K to 3K per year on top of a salary.

Salary of a Software Tester in the USA

I know little about salaries in the USA. All I know is based on people I know and network with from my blog and LinkedIn who work and live in America.

People working as Software Testers in the United States can earn an average of $55000 US dollars per year. Extra income, bonus or/and benefits for Software Testers can range from around $7000 US dollars to $8000 US dollars. Depending on experience, region, organization and set of skills salaries can range from $33000 US dollars to roughly $87000 US dollars.

Reference: *Salary Statics (UK)* | *itjobswatch.co.uk* | *https://goo.gl/KpW57u*

4. A Typical Working Day of a Software Tester

In everyday life of a Software Tester, a set of skills are required to accomplish the tasks daily. As a Software Tester, not every day are the same.

For a start, a typical day is a 7 hours work (plus lunch break) ranging from 9 am to 5 pm, but as no project are the same, it can vary on pre-release and on the actual development life cycle of a solution. It's common the releases happen outside of working hours, meaning, do expect to work early hours or even weekends in every major version. Some places do every two weeks, some areas do monthly, or sometimes within a range of every two months.

If you are lucky enough to work on a DevOps methodology using CI/CD (Meaning Continuous Integration / Continuous Deployment) it may be different as the approach to a release is different and the idea is that deployments can be done more often but at any time.

Communication

A software tester has to face constant challenges in communication. It's a continuous analysis of requirements to meet the acceptance criteria, identifying testable scenarios, impact analysis and gap analysis, taking workshops with Business Owners, Business Users, with the help of a BA

(Business Analysts) and other stakeholders as PM (Project Manager), PO (Product Owner), Developers and System Admin. It can be internal or external users who will use the software as the project progresses and get the releases throughout the development life cycle, meaning, getting the solution deployed into Dev environment, then into System Test environment, sometimes shared with Dev, then UAT environment when business users can test with the support of test analysts, then into Pre Production and finally into Production. To complete the cycle a smoke test or sanity checks are required with early life support then handed over to the BAU team.

A typical day for testers requires focus on a set of different activities. The investigation, preparation and planning are some of the key elements to prepare for when it comes to the actual test activity. So, expect to have much conversations, asking the questions, taking notes to understand the system and what the intentions are; as part of a tester investigation, asking questions and gathering information from various vital people is a crucial element of a successful tester.

Tester in Action

Once you have discussed around the objectives, you are then ready to go ahead and test. That is the system available to test. Developers carry out the deployment from their local machine into the DEV environment. Developers carry out what's called "unit tests," once it's successful, developers will then deploy to a test environment, called in most places, SIT (System Integration Test) or System Test environment. At this point testers can start the tests.

To begin the test run, the testers use the pre-identified test scenarios using the test cases written based on the requirements (also called user stories) that were previously read and understood in conjunction with the conversations with stakeholders.

Once all the acceptance criteria are met and the tests are successful, any diversion encountered or malfunction is identified; and the issue is discussed with the team. A bug must be logged with a clear description of steps to reproduce and screenshots/video, then added to the backlog of a management tool the team use. The developer gets a message to act on the defect and work towards the fix, and does the debug based on the given information. Once fixed, it is then deployed again into the test environment and testers re-test it. Once the tester is happy with the results, then the bug is closed with the test evidence (screenshot or video) attached to it.

Estimation and time management are essential once a test run has started. Ideally, it should get completed for the test batch within the allocated working hours.

In other words, you got to get your time estimation and effort as close to estimated time as possible; including investigation, preparation, actual test effort, reporting bugs and retests from when a bug is reported to returned as fixed from the development team. A good estimation comes with experience. Don't worry if you don't get it right at the beginning, but make sure you learn it along the way as this can be a demonstration to attention to the details and is an essential part of a Test Analyst professional career.

Timing

The tricky part in daily tasks is when bugs cleared in time, you are unable to retest. Only you can close a bug you have raised, because of that it's your responsibility to verify what you have identified, and for that reason, you depend on a successful fix from the development team.

There are instances, depending on the importance and impact of a bug, in which a bug is deferred to another phased release as it can be classed as low priority, also called *trivial*. When there's an understanding of not offering a significant impact in the system, this helps the team focus on the high critical defects towards meeting a deadline for the project milestone cycle.

An issue raised (AKA bug) must have a clear message. It has to have a good summarised title, a good description with steps to reproduce, a screenshot or video of where it was found and what data was used, and also a note of the environment and test user accounts you've used.

Testers must be prepared, at times, there's the need to move back and forth along with development teams to retest and close a bug. This is because, sometimes, more clarification is required adding to the bug description. This is to help developers understand the bug so they can fix it completely.

In Summary

As you can see, there are a few critical tasks and responsibilities that are required in the everyday work of tester.

So, the working hours for a Software Tester may be from 9 am to 5 pm, but their main goal is to complete the daily tasks and close all test cases assigned for the day. A software tester job is not easy because it requires time management, planning, communication, preparation, attention to details, reporting and focus. So, if you want to become a Tester, then take this scenario described into consideration.

I love what I do because no day is the same, and no project is the same. Every day, there's something new to uncover and report.

5. Expectations from a Software Tester Job

Software Testing is an essential part of the quality, verification and validation of a solution in development. This is to provide confidence that it has the quality and the value a product is expected to have.

Testers mainly conduct the manual and automation tests to help identify potential bugs and therefore minimize the impact of a fail, interacting between the developers and end users so developers can debug and fix any issues before the release to production, which is also called *live environment*.

Testers can work alongside with the developers while the software is developed or tested in a testing environment after the developer deploys the solution in a separate environment dedicated for testing, ideally with as close as possible to mimic the production version so testers can perform an exploratory test with the intention to identify any undesirable behaviour.

Psychology in Software Testing

It is known that for new IT graduates who are not fully confident about their coding skills while seeking for a job, someone usually suggests working as a software tester. It could be perhaps a stereotype that a piece of career advice may encourage the newly graduated to consider choosing Software Testing as a career. It may appear to others that this particular job is relatively easy to get into and won't need any advanced technical skills in comparison with programming.

However, it is quite the opposite. On top of having the technical knowledge and willingness to learn, Software

Testing requires a lot more than that to be a successful tester. Someone who will come into a project and provides value to the team.

Testers give a different perspective to the development; it sees it from a different angle. The goal of a Software Tester is to find bugs meaning, the assumption is, in most cases, is that it does not work and in preparation to prove it, testers have a conversation with everyone involved to understand what the business want. Considering the logic behind it, testers set themselves in a journey of exploration, discover, trial and error, looking for possible routes the user would take and try to uncover the mistakes and fails a bug introduced may cause, prior to the release of the product into the market.

In the end, Software Testers are as much responsible for the failure as the team in development, if the item is neglected. In the event of a failed item developed into an issue, the first question from the product owner and project management team is: Who has tested this and how it was tested?

Any test coverage that is missed by the tester accidentally may prompt to a disastrous result of the product created for the organization. Fundamental best practices and a proactive attitude is required to be a successful tester.

Being analytical is equally important as having technical skills; having more skills is better.

Communication

Being a Software Tester will involve, in most companies, working on a variety of different projects, being able to have excellent writing skills to write the test scripts, the interpretation of requirement analysis, and how you pass the information on in a bug description are essential skills. Also, you got to think about how you would interpret a meeting update, or an issue being described by the users, and those can make a big difference in the test.

As you start executing the test plan, you are prioritizing what is more important to test first and not forgetting key elements behind, liaising with the technical teams through the full development life cycle to UAT testing.

Must be able to work on your initiative and have excellent communication skills. You will have to ask the questions, be able to talk to anyone, directly or indirectly, involved with the development; with the business users, understanding their processes; and also, with the suppliers, sometimes with offshore team, and any other people.

Availability of the Job

In any software development projects, testing is an essential part of the process and is becoming more and more critical as we've seen an increase in the past years. There are constant changes in a short space of time, continually improving and regular new features being released due to the rapid innovation in technology and competition.

There's plenty of Software Testing jobs available, and you fulfil the demand by having the skills that match what is trending and the solution to the problems that companies are seeking.

It is vital to make yourself valuable by gaining knowledge on what is trending and what is happening in the market, getting more involved with the team, discussing with groups at work or testers groups and see what is going on out there.

In my experience, no project is the same; and there's always something new being used by someone, somewhere, and by being inquisitive, curious, proactive, you will gain more knowledge about the topic you are involved in, thus positioning you as an expert in the field. And when the right moment comes along you will be prepared and stand out from the crowd.

Only you set the limits.

The flexibility of the job

A typical job, a full-time permanent job is like any other; a 9-to-5 Monday to Friday.

Some companies offer more flexible hours, allowing you to start earlier or start late according to your circumstances.

Some allow you to work from home some days of the week.

In all circumstances, there are moments that you may need to go beyond those core hours due to a release, database migration or any other significant impact that a statement, hotfix or soft release may require. Sometimes, it could be an early start or even weekends. It all depends on the line of business you are involved in.

Some places allow a portion of your time, that in percentage including holidays, off sick paid days, recreation days, the charity paid days as part of the package, depending on the company you work with as a permanent.

Opposed to freelancers and contractors (consultants) who will only get paid when working and delivering milestones agreed.

6. Qualifications Needed for a Software Tester

A software tester is responsible for an essential part of software development. Testers are the quality assurance specialists who place themselves in the clients' and users' shoes. In a way, being the client advocate to everyone involved, and anticipating who the solution/web app/software will fit for purpose and as expected. Testers help to build confidence in the development cycle; checking and confirming development is on the right path.

Courses for Software Tester Job

Software testing job, like any other job in technology, requires a minimum qualification. The qualification can be in the form of a degree in computer science or any analytical background.

There are cases, such as business users, due to the work experience transition into software testing. Obtaining a certification in the field, such as **ISTQB**[1] foundation, can help you get into software testing.

Recent graduates can get a junior role and the more experienced can get straight to a test analyst role. It very much depends on the circumstances the tester is in.

There are places where you can specifically get skills to build up your knowledge in testing, to cover the certification, the manual tests, the automation tests, the performance tests, and many more. A place I like to get my skills up to date is **Udemy**[2], but there are other places like **Skillshare**[3] and **LinkedIn Learning**[4].

Software Testing Training

If you are interested in getting into the software testing job, you can exploit some free starter courses accessible online as long as you have Internet access. The **Microsoft Learn**[5] (formal MVA - Microsoft Virtual Academy) provides excellent online courses, offers the fundamental and beginners basic courses, in particular tools that you may end up using to manage the test plan such as **Azure DevOps**[6] and to help understand the **Azure Cloud Services**[7], so you are prepared when a job requiring this particular knowledge presents itself to you.

Also, the online site of **ASTQB**[8] (American Software Testing Qualifications Board) has introduced its syllabus covering a range of detailed software testing path you can choose depending on the type of skill you wish to pursue, available in the PDF to download so you can study on your own and plenty of questionnaires to practice and test your learning progress.

Other Courses

If you wish to get a job in software testing and don't have any related degree mentioned above, then the focus on getting the foundation certification such as ISTQB or ASTQB. This is the minimum to help you understand the development life cycle and where the testing fits in. Getting the certification alone can increase your chances to get your dream job. Check out my preparation for the **ISTQB course**[9] in Udemy and **Skillshare**[10].

It would be best if you were Teachable

What do I mean by that? It is the fact that we are all constantly learning, and we must be open to it in any circumstances or project you are in. As part of the success concept, I mentioned embedded here in these teachings is the **Teachability Index***.

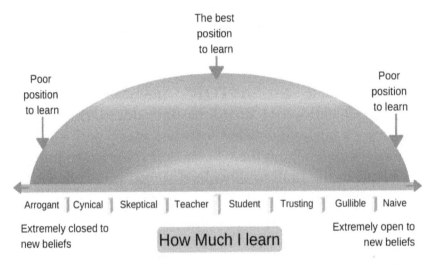

In summary, it is the willingness to change and to learn. It would be best if you considered this at all times.

This is the change in way of seeing the 'I get it' as opposed to 'I am getting it' is a constant, not a definitive; otherwise, you will become unteachable.
There are two dimensions on a scale of 1 to 10.

Willingness-to-learn

Time, money & effort you're willing to invest (i.e., waking up 4:30 in the morning, buying the right training courses, sticking to the end)

What are you willing to give up in order to learn this material? (i.e., Not watching TV for weeks)

Willingness-to-accept-change

You got to ask those simple questions:
"Are you happy with where you are at?"

If your answer is on the lines of:
"I'll do whatever it takes to learn this" then you are on the right path.

Once I've heard this line, it stuck with me, and I believe it is applicable in everything we do:
"If you want things in your life to change, then you have to change things in your life."

You are insane if you do the same things on and on and expect different results, and you must do things differently.

Putting simply, you are going to have to change the way you think if you want to succeed in whatever you are pursuing; in this instance, the top high-end paying software testers that everyone wants to have in their team project.

If you want to become valuable, you have to use these simple concepts, if you choose to. It has worked and is continuously working for me.

References:

[1]*ISTQB:* istqb.org
[2]*Udemy:* bit.ly/2Vl0nuu
[3]*Skillshare:* skl.sh/2vNRRF6 *(2 months **free**)*
[4]*LinkedIn Learning:* bit.ly/37br5qV *(30 days **free**)*
[5]*Microsoft Learn:* docs.microsoft.com/en-us/learn
[6]*Azure DevOps:* azure.microsoft.com/en-gb/services/devops/
[7]*Azure Cloud Services:* azure.microsoft.com/en-gb/features/azure-portal/
[8]*ASTQB:* astqb.org
[9]*ISTQB Prep Course:* bit.ly/2DWM58W
Coursera: bit.ly/2HaEF3J *(7 days **trial**)*

Disclosure: *Some of the links within here are affiliate links, meaning, **at NO additional cost to you**, I will earn a commission if you click through and make a purchase. I do this in aim to help support me with developing more great content for you and others.*

*Teachability Index, the concept is not new, and is widely known from The Global Information Network, in the series 'Your Wish is Your Command', though by Kevin Trudeau a former 33-degree member of the secret society The Brotherhood, it has been used by many people to achieve anything people wanted.

7. Skills needed for a Software Tester

If you want to get into a quality assurance software testing field, then you need to have a clear view of what it takes to be a successful tester.

In these days, with fast-paced technology changes, the software testing industry changes fast. The number of people looking to get a placement is increasing as this field has become more and more popular as the year goes by.

The need to get excellent quality applications has become a trending topic and organizations are recognising the need for testing input in the development life cycle. Equally, the demand for good testers is also increasing.

To get into software testing, an individual will need to have some particular set of skills.

Skills a Tester Should Have

A software tester should have the capacity to create sufficient scenarios (test cases) depending on what the aim is. The testers should place themselves in the clients' shoes and apply every possible scenario to cover sufficient situations in the workflow process of the application to flush out any anomalies.

A tester should aim to understand the system as much as possible: how to use it, installing, setting up, and perform the test cases based on a previous analysis in the test case preparation.

Testers should have at least a general knowledge of how data basis work, ideally interrogating the database to be able to verify the data entered and the output areas desired.

One of the essential skills a software tester should have is the capacity to adjust and learn rapidly.

Testers should know testing principles based on ISTQB standards.

Testers should own the testing aspect and be in constant communication with the development team, raising any concerns, risks and defects, and should be able to confront and interact positively with others to get the best quality software out to production.

Additional skills of Software Tester

One of the best tester skills to have is the capacity to look in different ways to find defects and errors in the system and its processes, and you may need to be creative and go beyond the usual using the system and exploring all the possible options available.

To help achieve the right level of work, being enthusiastic gives a feeling of self-achievement when reaching milestones. To be a successful software tester, the individual needs to be passionate about what they do and what the project entails. Show interest and engage with others within the team and the users to help keep you motivated throughout the development cycle.

To have a successful test run, the planning is essential; so when executing, having all in place with the satisfaction to be able to run what was planned is good. Covering positive and negative test will surely cover all that is needed to gain the level of confidence the team needs to succeed with the release.

Don't be personal, don't limit yourself to present the facts; be diplomatic and don't let other people's opinions get to you. Stick with the principles and produce reports to reflect that.
Have a track record of all the communication, including email, instant messages, screenshots, data output, videos, and many more, to help support with your tests and for auditing purposes.

I recommend a workshop with the users once the test phase is complete. Record the screen as well and save as an asset so others can later use as a guide if they need to.
Have a good mental health practice to be up to the challenging days and in down times, review your test templates, so you are always prepared.

8. Work Experience of a Software Tester

While software tester experience, abilities and skill set are focusing on technical skills and qualifications, other factors need to be considered in the journey of a quality assurance services provider. The soft skills are equally required to successfully become a professional tester helping to provide value to the project, the team and the organisation whom testers are working with.

Technical Skills

Constant technical skill update is required. I'd suggest focusing on what's most relevant at the moment, with the project and the work stack tools that you are involved with as the variants are in hundreds, if not in thousands to choose to learn. (Go back to Chapter 6 - **'Qualifications Needed for a Software Tester'** - so you can refer to places to acquire specific training related to that particular area you want to learn).

The combination of the technical skills with the soft skills, such as being able to communicate well; being able to investigate and ask questions; being able to persuade and guide users to help with the information you need; to help cover as much as you can combining with the requirements; acceptance criteria, and solution design can help.

Soft Skills

In addition to that, being a team player, being the bridge between the development team and the users, facilitating any conversation that helps clarifying any gaps, misunderstanding and ambiguous information, can demonstrate experience and it comes with more and more exposure. The more you do, the more you get the experience around that topic.

As you gather that information and physically test the scenarios in question, you will need to report the progress, with the project team; raising any defects and concerns along the way and that means you will talk to the users, to reproduce the issue and validate the defect according with the project objectivity and with the Project Manager and the Developers to understand the risks, impact and priority to solve that particular issue matching with the bigger picture. That would have a positive effect in being able to progress ahead with the milestones and deadlines goals.

You have to manage the expectations in yourself, the users and the development team. Avoid exhaustive testing and anything that is not the objective by identifying what's out of scope.

There's a saying that anybody can do testing, but can anybody see the bigger picture?

The product team could ask only users to test the system, but due to lack of understanding and experience in software testing under the development life cycle, it almost certainly will only cover the functionality of the system, covering maybe only, known as the 'happy path'.

That's when experience comes to place; individuals with the right mentality towards testing and knowledge around this subject can get an effective result in the tests. I am not saying to use the users; they are essential as well. What I'm saying is, do not neglect the need of professional, experienced testers in the development project.

A tester can in this instance guide and support the users in the UAT (User Acceptance Testing) phase, providing a timescale, coverage, environment access, test user accounts, data, test plan, test approach and manage the defect log; being the bridge between the technical team and the business/users and that comes with experience. The more you are exposed to those scenarios, the more experience you get and more successful you will be.

Psychology of Testing

One thing I've learned and once I understood this bit, things became more and more enjoyable, that is, we are in a project to help…help to solve problems. We are in with an objective, gathering information to help solve those problems. We are not in to express our feelings and opinions on how people work, but simply present the facts to the team so we can collectively focus on solving the issues.

Okay. You will along the way encounter people from different backgrounds, experience and mind-sets, but you are not to be drawn into their beliefs and personal opinions. Don't let a negative comment get into you and the way you work. Once you apply the principles and defend the need to cover the critical task of a tester, this is all that matters; and that comes with experience.

Look after your mental health and beliefs as this will give you grounds when facing difficult times and challenging people while working in projects. It is a team effort and if you stand your ground and talk to people, these issues can be overcome.

Help seek ways out of the problem, help to find options, adding value to the team with a different perspective of thinking when discussing an issue and its issues.

That's what we are in this for: to solve problems. The more you tackle the issues, the sooner you do, the better it would be to get a solution. The attitude towards it makes much difference, and you will help others in the team plus inspire others to do the same.

In life I've learned that we will never please 100% of people. Focus on doing the right thing and the people that matter the most will be pleased and satisfied; the rest are all noises that you and the project can live with.

In Conclusion

To conclude, I'd say it's 50/50:

50% - Technical skills - work experience
50% - Soft Skill and mental health - life experience

This is clearly identified in job interviews, and there are times you walk into an interview and have a balance of 50/50 or 80/20 on both ways. Sometimes you feel like all the discussion was around technical skills and other cases all the conversation was around the soft skills. You would be able to pick up where it's heading as the interview goes along.

9. Sectors Software Testers Can Work With

Just like any other occupations, getting in Software Testing and choosing this profession requires time management; the ability to work on your initiative; discipline; enthusiasm; and focus, to begin with. If you do not have these in mind, chances are that you will get frustrated rapidly, which will negatively affect the execution of your work and the product item under test.

That's a fact, but a fact can be misleading. There are different sectors, and that can directly affect how you will work and how the project is handled. There are sectors in which testers are more evident and there are sectors that testers are not so evident.

The riskier the project is, the more you are going to exercise your skills.

Let's say it is a related finance system or a life-threatening system that needs to get tested. It will require more thorough testing, which means, a more experienced and qualified tester is needed, and more significant expectations are needed from you and the work you are about to deliver.

It is a system that won't have a significant impact financially or in somebody's life, such as eCommerce or a supply chain logistics company or a training package, for example, maybe the less pressure a tester will get. However, that doesn't mean you won't have to do a thorough work; as a defect system can lead to loss of reputation and loss of revenue, in some cases data breaches can legally affect the order and the company you are going to be working with.

Some sectors you are potentially be working with are:

Retail	Public Sector
Health	Technology
Automotive	Finance / Banking
Supply Chain / Logistic	Transportation
eCommerce	Education

The Asking

As a minimum requirement for you to be able to get into one of the sectors mentioned here is that you follow the fundamentals of testing, which means some recruiters don't even consider calling you for an interview if you are not ISTQB certified. (More details in Chapter 6 - **Qualifications Needed for a Software Tester**).

However, some interviewers will consider interviewing you if you don't have the certification, based on your experience. For example, if you are an expert in CRM, or any particular tool. I happen to be an experienced tester in Microsoft Dynamics 365 and ERP Agresso form Unit 4 and Gigatron ERP (a Brazilian ERP SaaS company) and all the contract project consultancy work I've provided, none of them asked for my ISTQB certification.

The interview can be purely based on the experience and around how the communication is expected to be (notice that is mostly around the soft skills).

The focus on testing can be more around the business processes and the communication with the business users. This is essential. A lot of the functions are customised, meaning understanding how a particular process works can help immensely in achieving the end goal.

These days companies are directly recruiting or have a supplier of software testing services, you can contact them directly with your CV and a covering letter. Some companies' websites provide a contact us facility to send out the interest to work for them; some don't. I suggest researching each one of them and contact them directly.

Equally, I can say about how it works in the UK; maybe it's similar in USA, Canada, Australia and New Zealand. There are specialist recruiters who help to find talents for companies and consultancy companies.

The offers could be in the format of:

Permanent basis - Ranging from Junior to Senior. Where you work for the company and receive all the benefits of being a permanent employee from that company. Basic annual salary.

Fixed-term - Senior role. It can be a 12 month-contract, with similar benefits and salary of a permanent position. Basic annual salary.

Short-term contract - It is an expert and experienced senior tester. It is also called "contractor," "freelancer" or "consultant". It is based more on the project delivery, that can vary from 1 to 3 months and the possibility of an extension offered after that. It can range from 1 month rolling, or 3 or 6 months, in my experience. It almost always gets an expansion in the contract mostly 3 or 6 months. Paid on a daily rate basis.

The people who will contact you are:

Agency recruiters - It's a dedicated agency recruiter company whose main services are searching and finding people, providing the pre-interview and finding the individual for the company looking to fulfil the role. Could be permanent or contractual position;

Talent recruiters - Those are people from under the HR team in an organisation who will not use the services of an Agency Recruiter to find the talented person to work permanently;

Consultancy recruiters - A recruiter who works for a consultancy company looking for someone to work for them on a permanent role and being outsourced as contract role for their clients. You could work on a range of customers and could be a reasonable basis if you ever intend to go for consulting in future.

Consultancy Companies

Here are some large consultancy companies who are in a constant lookout for people to help their clients with the testing. Ideal if you want to make a start looking for a job right away.

myExpert.Solutions	Zenstar
TCS	HP
IBM	Hexaware

Infosys

SQS Group

Capgemini

QA Source

QA Mentor

Test Matick

QualiTest Group

uTest

Cognizant

TestingXperts

TestFort

Wipro

Performance Lab

Stresstesters.com

Acutest

Sogeti

And many more. I recommend that you search the ones more relevant to you and your local area.

Working Remotely Job Posts

Bear in mind that there are options these days to work remotely and there are other places where you can search for remote work as a freelancer or even permanently.

Here are just a few:

Snap.hr - bit.ly/2HadHIb
Working Nomads - bit.ly/2WxuOtT
Remote.co - bit.ly/2VprQeF

Prepare

My suggestion is to get your CV ready.
I was hoping you could read my blog post on **5 Tips to Get a Job Through LinkedIn** (bit.ly/2VqziGl)

When you search for a job in software testing, if you are starting and getting into this field, search for keywords like, 'Junior Tester', 'Junior Test Analyst', 'Test Analyst'.

Once you find a job, read the specifications and what it is that they are asking. When writing the covering letter, mention the areas that you can help based on the job description.

When you get a call, or straight to the interview, use that as an experience to build up your knowledge and consequently your confidence.

Don't get into the negatives of not being recruited in your first, second or third interview, understand that you are getting more and more experienced in the interviews, and soon you will see a pattern on how the questions are, and you will be able to answer more and more confidently as more interviews you get.

I'm a believer of as so many "no's" we get; closer we are getting to a "yes".

Remember, as I mentioned before, you can never please 100% of people. Focus on the ones that matter the most.

Keep on doing it, and eventually, you are going to get it. Persistence is the key. Never give up.

10. How to Find a Job in Software Testing?

Once you've reviewed your CV and researched some places where you want to contact the potential location, as mentioned in the previous chapter, proceed as follows.

If you are graduating, seek to get the ISTQB certification, then look for jobs in the junior level to get into the field and gain experience.

You should have received some guidance from career advice and job interview workshop event days by now.

If you are changing careers and want to get into the field, search for entry-level job posts or within your company. Ask the IT department team if there are any openings and if someone can talk to you about the possibilities to have a trial in the department. Trust me when I say this, but the IT team needs help from experienced users and having someone in the team who understands how the business and its processes works, is valuable. Make yourself useful, letting them know that you are interested in knowing more about how to bridge between your area and IT.

Search for local agencies and make the initial contact. These days via the Internet first, through their website, but I strongly suggest searching in LinkedIn as recruiters are most active there.

DM the Recruiters and Ask the Question

> "Hi, I'm interested in finding out more about how to get into software testing.
> Can you help me?
> I have attached my CV and my work experience.
> Let me know when it is an excellent time to have a chat?
> Thank you.
> Rogerio da Silva
> Mobile: +44777123456
> Email: email@rogeriodasilva.com "

Social media can be an add-on factor to today's modern job seeker.

However, I would stick to LinkedIn to begin with, as it is the leading recruiters' platform and more related to jobs. It is a place where you can showcase your experience and competencies. I'm amazed how there are people who are still not taking the full advantage of it.

I am not saying to avoid all the other social media platforms. I use almost all of them, but there are contents with a different format, messages and expectations in each one of them.

All this information can help you build up the knowledge and the confidence in looking for a job.

Bonus Point

There's one thing I've learned that helped and helped me every day. I want to share with you here just a fraction of what it is, but I believe it can improve on the search.

It's a concept called **Training Balance Scale***.

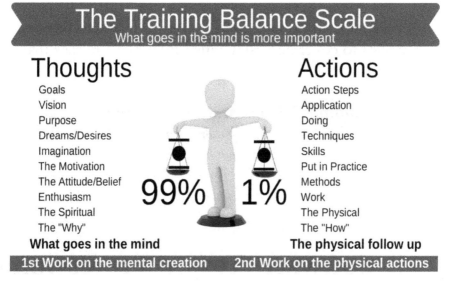

The one side of the scale: What goes on inside of your mind? The "why" is what you think and feel.

Thoughts, desires, dreams, goals, attitude, mental process, objectives, vibration, intention, energy, emotions and motivation

The other side of the balance scale: Is what you do: the "How"

Actions, movements, techniques, strategies, action steps, plans, activities, physical actions

Which means you must focus on what you want, on what your desires are, and on the 'thinking' part of the process. Don't focus on the 'how' to begin with, then how is just a percentage of the result.

I'm planning to expand more about this in future material; just a lot to cover here, stay tuned for when I release that as well.

The Training Balance Scale concept is not new, and is widely known from The Global Information Network, in the series 'Your Wish is Your Command', though by Kevin Trudeau a former 33-degree member of the secret society The Brotherhood, it has been used by many people to achieve anything people wanted.

11. Software Tester Professional Development

More and more people who have chosen software testing as a career are benefiting a good salary, and there are expert consultants out there earning six figures today. That's a fact.

To be able to get to that point, the software tester must prepare him/herself by thinking about career development and having a clear view of the path he/she chooses to take.

The natural starting path is the certification; the most known one is ISTQB foundation level, which provides information and support the way a person would desire; being more technical-, more business- or more people-oriented.

Starting from the Foundation Level, you could choose the path to work mostly in the methodology the team will be working on, for example, Agile Tester.

Alternatively, if you prefer working in the core of testing, then becoming a Test Manager or a Technical Specialist on Automation, Security or Performance and many more specific areas of testing, is more probable.

Here's an ISTQB[R] (International Software Testing Qualifications Board) illustration of the paths you can choose:

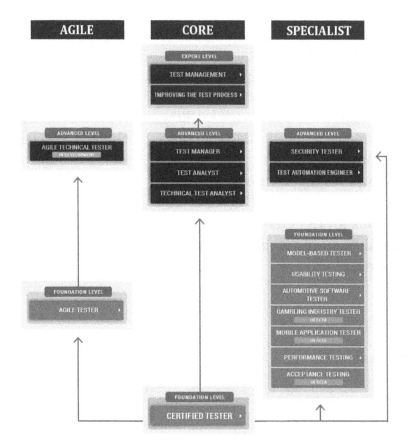

ISTQB Certification: Be a Professional Software Tester!

An ISTQB Certification is a recognised certification for program testing. This certificate can be taken through a recognised testing Exam Provider by its Member Boards. An Exam Provider is an association authorized by a Member Boards to offer exams locally as well as globally, which also includes online testing certification. Applicants who effectively pass the exam are given the certificate of ISTQB Certified Tester.

This site provides all the minimum necessary training material, which is essential to help you pass the ISTQB exam of any chosen level.

The certificate for the professional tester is available in almost 70 countries, and it is one of the most recognised certificates, just a few essential facts to consider are:

The ISTQB certificate can be taken in a local recognised test centre and is an online web application.

It does not require any work experience.

It can be quickly taken up by anybody from IT as well as the non-IT field.

It is recognized worldwide, and it's the quickest process on certification for a software tester in the world.

This certification can get you qualified to work in anyplace and anywhere in the world.

ISTQB certificate never expires. It will remain valid forever. To get the recognition that you deserve as a professional tester, you should get certified; and trust me, is not that hard to get.

Agile Methodology

If you are serious about becoming ISTQB certified, a tester who understands the Agile methodology can help you with getting and retaining the contract work in comparison to others who don't know how to work in this methodology. I'm not going to get into details here; I'll let you do your research, but I'll promise to provide more material around this methodology and others equally crucial as this called Waterfall model (a bit obsolete but there are companies who are still using it) and V-Model, which is covered in a bit more detail within the ISTQB syllabus, and I'll expand more on that in future materials.

Knowing Agile methodology is beneficial for a software tester; some of the reasons are listed below:

- It happens in a fast-paced environment and customers see the value testers are adding to the project much faster.

- Testers have better interactions with customers. Users, clients, designers, developers, product owners, business analysts, project manager and testers; everyone interacts with each other.

A working program is delivered in small chunks, much quicker. i.e. weeks instead of months.

Discussions are, in most cases, face-to-face.

Regular catch up via stand-ups, "what did you do yesterday? What are your plans for today? Have you got any blockers?" across the team, so everyone is aware of what everyone is working on at that time.

Indeed, even late changes in the requirements are invited and put on the table
These are some of the main advantages of Agile methodology and as a software tester it's essential to understand how it works as it directly affects your performance as you develop and expand your successful career in this field.

The Four Steps Process to Learn a New Information

To conclude the four concepts mentioned throughout this book and is entirely applicable when it comes to the time that you are processing a new piece of information, use this framework concept.

The Analogy: There was a time that you didn't know how to do your shoelaces. Then you were thought about how to do it. Then you learned how to do it and knew how to.

Now you do that automatically as you've done it so many times that you don't even realise doing it. Do you recall doing your shoelaces today?

Do you recall driving back in or back from work if you use the same commute route every day?

What I'm saying is, you didn't know that you didn't know and now that you know it's all in autopilot.

In life, we can do the same and achieve that; but repetition, by listening and doing it over and over and over again.

So, make the most of the videos, audios and contents that you acquire. Practice, early in the morning before you set off to work; while you are commuting; when you return home, switch off the TV for a while and practice.

The more you do, the more it gets imprinted in your subconscious mind and like magic, the autopilot kicks in and you do it naturally.

In summary, if you read this and keep this in mind, while referring to every time you learn a piece of new information, and keep on practising, it will help you immensely to succeed in your Software Testing career. I've done, many others before me have, and I'm sure it will help you too as this is a universal law and applies to anyone and anywhere in the world.

The four steps for when you are processing a piece of new information are:

- Unconscious Incompetence
  - You don't know what you don't know
  - You see the info but have to apply the info consciously

- Conscious Incompetence
  - You know what you don't know

- Conscious Competence
  - You know what you know

- Unconscious Competence – **This is the ultimate objective. You want to get to this point.**
  - You know, and it happens automatically
  - Manifesting your desires at record speed

12. Career Prospects of a Software Tester

Software Testing in a more analyst level or also called Quality Assurance in a more strategic level are going through a constant transformation. There is a continuous increase in demand, in new tools and techniques. As you get more experienced, you will be asked to go beyond your zone of comfort; but trust me when I say this, with the right attitude towards being open to learning, having the curiosity approach, and by trial and error, you can become a tremendous successful tester.

In my experience and others in the field that I know, we recognise that and understand the fact that to be successful in this field, you have to be open-minded and always think about giving value to the project team delivery, to the project, and to the product owner.

If we are transparent enough, we will contribute to the level of confidence in the developed product solution. With a clear message and a clear understanding, we will succeed.

If you're a recent graduate or an experienced tester, this will apply to both; the only difference is the salary and the self-confidence. Do your homework; learn the basics I mentioned here throughout the book; and my secrets (that aren't so secret and I did not invent but borrow), learned, understood, and applied; and now passing on to you so you can do and be the same.

The laws of nature are equally distributed to all of us, and we need to understand and tap on that and leverage what is available to us.

Learn the basics, the four basics are:

- Who do you listen to?
- Teachability Index
- Training / Balance Scale
- Four steps to processing new information
- Master the first four basics / Focus on the fundamentals

The concept is applicable not just for software testing; it happens that I have used it here, but it can well apply to anyone and anywhere in any situation.

So, no matter if you're working as an engineer software tester, lead or manager tester, as long as you are responsible for your actions and being accountable for your attitudes, you will surely get the success you deserve.

If the nature is working under the universal laws, there will be more career prospects for you if you are doing your job right.

If you are a fresh graduate, you have to take up some well-recognized testing certifications like ISTQB to increase career prospects in software testing.

If you have any other certifications or skills, there will be more chances of a great start for your career.

Career prospects for an individual going through a bachelor's in Computers or studying anything related to technology or computer/programming may be outstanding more in comparison to those who are not studying these subjects. However, there are cases of people in different backgrounds getting into the fields as well, so don't use this a blockage for you.

With other related areas of testing, once you have the fundamental certification, other testing certificates are also the key for the chosen career. They will increase the chances of a fantastic job, and you will surely get many benefits.

So, in the testing career, excellent skills, well-recognized testing certifications, software testing training or some experience. If you have any of these, then you have a bright future in this career, and you will surely get success in software testing.

Conclusion

Well, if you have got to the end, well done.

There is so much information there, and I feel like I'm only scratching the surface.

I hope I have sparked your curiosity to know more in the pursuit of the software testing field consulting business.

I have laired out information in my own experience throughout the years, combining the technical skills, following the fundamental software testing principals with the soft skills learned in life with the four fundamental concepts I have embedded within this material. I hope you have noticed that.

In summary, before you decide which route to take (as permanent work or contractor) and which expertise you want to pursue in software testing basing in the ISTQB route (Manual Tester, Automation Tester, Test Manager, Agile Tester, Performance and Security Tester), and whichever direction you will have to put effort and get the best you can to succeed successfully, I would suggest mastering the basics and here are the basics.

#1 Who do you listen to?

Find the person that you are inspired to be. Copy everything that he does and says. Ask for advice, get mentoring if that option is available. Read, eat and brief that model.

#2 Teachability Index

Ask yourself these questions:

How teachable are you?

How is your willingness to learn and do things differently?

How open are you to accept change and to do things differently?

What are you willing to give up?

What are you willing to invest in time and money?

If you want things in your life to change, then you have to change things in your life.

#3 The Training Balance Scale

One side of the scale is what goes inside your mind, how you think and feel, the "**WHY**".

Thoughts	Thinking
Desires	Dreams
Goals	Attitude
Mental Processes	Objectives
Vibration	Intention
Energy	Emotions
Motivation	

The other side of the scale is what you do; the "**HOW**".

Actions	Movements
Techniques	Strategies
Action Steps	Plans
Activities	Physical Actions

#4 The Four Steps to Process New Information

- Unconscious Incompetence
  - You don't know what you don't know
  - You see the info but have to apply the info consciously

- Conscious Incompetence
  - You know what you don't know

- Conscious Competence
  - You know what you know

- Unconscious Competence – **This is the main objective. You want to get to this point.**
  - You know, and it happens automatically
  - Manifesting your desires at record speed

Once you master those basics, going through the process of getting skilled in Software Testing is relatively easy as I believe insecurity can have a negative impact in your development. We deal with information, and we deal with people all the time. We must be confident of what we are doing at all times so we can help with the quality assurance, providing value for the project team helping to build the confidence the management leaders expect to get from us.

I don't think any of us, testers, even the experienced ones, do realise. That took me a while to understand that and once I started to apply those principles, my output doubled; the results doubles and my income tripled. Not many other testers are on six figures today, and I can say almost for sure that I can get a contract role anytime and anywhere I want.

I don't say this to brag but to show that you can do that too. If I can do it, so can you.

If you would like to work more closely and want to develop your career learning from experts in the field, with my team and I, stay tuned. I'll be sharing more details in my website, Facebook group and LinkedIn group.

I want to congratulate you for taking the next step, moving beyond mere personal growth and deciding to use your lessons to contribute to your success and others.

What matters the most is not how much money you make; it's how many lives you would impact with your services. The money is just a cool way to keep track of what's happening.

I realised that I did struggle with my past business for a couple of years because I was so scared about investing in myself. I was never able to ask other people to invest in the products and services I created and provided either. It wasn't until I started to make financial commitments with different coaches and mentors that I was finally able to become congruent.

Because I was investing in myself, I was able to go out and ask others to invest in themselves with my products and services.

I want to invite you to hang out with the other amazing like-minded people in my world and me. Spend time in the social media groups, watch our videos, come to our events, and make friends with other people like you.

I believe in the power of networking and exchanging experiences. There may be people in different fields, but I think they all have a similar mission: changing the world through quality assurance. That has been my driving force in the past six years, and I feel so blessed to have the chance to work with bright people within the same interests as you who is doing the exact same thing.

With that said, I encourage you to master the skills in this book. Become a master 'Jedi' in Software Consulting services. Become the vehicle for change that I know you can be.
After you've done that, I encourage you to go deeper. Spend more time with us and figure out how to take your services, your company, your business, and your customers life to the next level.

Thanks for spending this time with me. I'll talk to you soon.

Rogerio da Silva

PS: Remember, if I can do it, so can you.

References

Software Testing Books

'Secrets of a Buccaneer-Scholar: How Self-Education and the Pursuit of Passion Can Lead to a Lifetime of Success' Paperback– 3 Sep 2009 by James Bach (Author) - amzn.to/2HvjNDs

'User Acceptance Testing: A step-by-step guide' Kindle Edition by Brian Hambling (Author), Pauline van Goethem (Author) - amzn.to/2Vua4lO

'Software Testing: An ISTQB-BCS Certified Tester Foundation' guide 3rd Edition, Kindle Edition by Brian Hambling (Author, Editor), Peter Morgan (Author), Angelina Samaroo (Author), Geoff Thompson (Author), Peter Williams (Author) - amzn.to/2ZCz7H3

'Lessons Learned in Software Testing: A Context-Driven' Approach 1st Edition, Kindle Edition by Bret Pettichord (Author), Cem Kaner (Author), James Bach (Author) - amzn.to/2HntCTB

Life Changing Books

'How to Win Friends and Influence People' by Dale Carnegie - amzn.to/2E9HS1E

'How to Win Friends and Influence People in the Digital Age' by Dale Carnegie Training - amzn.to/2HsUQlw

'The Game of Work' by Charles A. Coonradt (Author), Lawrence V. Jackson (Foreword), Lee Nelson (Contributor) - amzn.to/2HtbhET

'See you at the top' by Zig Ziglar - amzn.to/2JHQJLt

'The Magic of Thinking Big' by David J. Schwartz - amzn.to/2JG17na

'New Psycho-cybernetics' by Maxwell Maltz - amzn.to/2LFQF1v

'What you say is what you get' by Don Gossett - amzn.to/2JktpUG

'Your Wish Is Your Command' 14 Disk Cd Set + Guidebook (Your Wish Is Your Command How To Manifest Your Desires - amzn.to/2WIATDX

Disclosure: *Some of the links within here are affiliate links, meaning,* **at NO additional cost to you,** *I will earn a commission*

if you click through and make a purchase. I do this in aim to help support me with developing more great content for you and others.

www.ingramcontent.com/pod-product-compliance
Lightning Source LLC
Chambersburg PA
CBHW071551080326
40690CB00056B/1793